THE ~~SOUL~~

OF

SUCCESS

4 POWERFUL L.E.A.P. STRATEGIES TO DOUBLE YOUR PROFITS

THE ~~SOUL~~

OF

SUCCESS

4 POWERFUL
L.E.A.P. STRATEGIES
TO DOUBLE YOUR PROFITS

SHAGUN BANGA

Worldwide Published by
Pendown Press

PENDOWN PRESS LLP
An ISO 9001 & ISO 14001 Certified Co.,
Regd. Office: 3767A, Kanhaiya Nagar,
Tri Nagar, Delhi-110035
Ph.: 8180886000, 9650072927, 8595249536
E-mail: info@pendownpress.com
Branch Office: 1A/2A, 20, Hari Sadan, Ansari Road,
Daryaganj, New Delhi-110002
Ph.: 011-45794768
Website: PendownPress.com

First Edition: 2023

ISBN: 978-93-5554-571-8

Dedicated to...

This book is dedicated to my father, Mr. Mohinder Kumar Banga, who has been the beacon throughout my journey. His wisdom and courage, alongside a relentless pursuit of excellence, have lit the way for me. The path I've taken is brighter because of him. His enduring influence echoes in every word and idea in this book.

Contents

Author Bio

With an extensive background in Mechanical Engineering and a proven track record in the sole moulding machine industry, Shagun Banga is a visionary entrepreneur and industry expert. Through years of experience, innovative thinking, and a customer-centric approach, Shagun has revolutionized the manufacturing landscape. His book serves as a valuable resource for businesses seeking to choose the ideal sole moulding machine, equipping them with the knowledge and guidance needed to make informed decisions. Shagun's passion for excellence and unwavering commitment to pushing the boundaries of technology continue to propel his company forward and shape the industry as a whole.

Education

- Shagun is a graduate in B.Tech in Mechanical Engineering.

- He holds certifications in simulation, machine design & 3D modelling using Solidworks CAD software.

- He is certified as an expert in Business Mastery Programme, Digital Marketing, and Overbooked Marketing Strategies.

Notably, he excels in Business Operations Automation, showcasing his ability to leverage technology for optimizing business processes. Additionally, he is a certified trainer in 'Spin-Selling' and 'Disc', demonstrating his profound understanding of sales techniques and behavioural assessments.

Experience

With over 21 years of experience, Shagun Banga serves as the Managing Director at Technocrat Mouldings Pvt. Ltd., a leading expert in Footwear machinery. Under his leadership, the company has successfully supplied over 1420 machines to more than 600 clients, solidifying its reputation for delivering high-quality products and exceptional service.

Achievements

In his 21-year journey, Mr. Banga, takes great pride in stating that their company was the pioneer in introducing these machines for the first time in India. Through their dedication and vision, they have played a significant role in bringing innovative technologies to the Indian market.

1. Single Color TPR Sole Static Machine in the year 1992.

2. TPR Sole Machine Book Winding type for Welt insert soles in the year 2005.

3. Double Color TPR Sole Static Machine in the year 2014.

4. Shoe Last Moulding Machine in the year 2017.

5. Insole Press machine. (Memory Foam and Socks) in the year 2019.

6. Eva Hot and Cold Rotary Machine in the year 2023.

Foreword

It is my immense privilege to present before you, "The Sole of Success," penned by Shagun. In an industry where margins are slim and competition is fierce, this book serves as a guiding light for footwear sole manufacturers.

This book focuses on the sole, which is a vital part of every shoe. It explains how to select the right machines for manufacturing soles, considering their strengths and weaknesses. By making astute decisions, manufacturers can be more efficient and productive.

The book will guide you on how to harness the power of the LEAP framework for maximum profitability. His principles on implementing the LEAP framework are not just ideas but well-tested strategies that have the power to revolutionize your business and lead you towards unprecedented profits.

Shagun's passion for footwear manufacturing shines through in his writing. He explains things clearly, making it easy for readers to understand. Whether you're a new entrepreneur, an established manufacturer, or just curious about the industry, "The Sole of Success" is a valuable resource to help you excel.

Harsh Sachdeva
Alert Group

Foreword

The sole of a shoe is an incredibly important part. It bears our weight, absorbs impact, and keeps us grounded. Understanding the significance of the sole, Shagun has written a remarkable book called "The Sole of Success" specifically tailored for footwear sole manufacturers. This book is all about helping them choose the right machines, improve their processes, and make more money.

In "The Sole of Success," Shagun generously shares his knowledge and offers practical advice that manufacturers can implement to achieve to success. He emphasizes the crucial role of selecting the best machines for sole production. By understanding the strengths and weaknesses of different machines, manufacturers can make smart decisions and be more efficient.

The book also focuses on making processes better. Shagun gives valuable tips on streamlining production and minimizing waste. He explains the importance of balancing costs and quality to make more profit. By following the strategies shared in this book, manufacturers can achieve better financial results.

Shagun's passion for footwear manufacturing resonates in his writing. He explains concepts clearly and in a way that is easy to understand. Whether you are just starting out in the business, already making soles, or simply curious about the industry, "The Sole of Success" is a valuable guide that can help you succeed.

Sunil Manchanda
Versatile Operations

Acknowledgements

To my brother, Shubham, whose unwavering camaraderie and insights have been my strength.

To my wife, Namrata, for her constant love, patience, and belief in my vision.

To my sister, Samiksha, for her encouragement and the joy she brings into every challenge we face.

To my mother, Mrs. Parveen, whose endless support and wisdom have shaped my character.

To my employees, for their dedication and hard work that transform challenges into triumphs.

To my clients, whose trust and feedback have been crucial in steering our collective success.

My Journey So Far...

In 1992, my father had a business of manufacturing recycled PVC granules. One day, he saw a costly Italian machine at a client's factory, and learned that it was too expensive for many businesses. But my dad got an idea – why not make a machine like that, but one we could all afford? So, my father decided to make a similar, affordable machine in India. It was tough because he wasn't a technical person, but after two years of hard work, he did it. Thanks to him, lots of small factories in India started to grow and do better.

Since my childhood, I saw my dad working really hard every single day. I saw all the tough times he went through and the great things he accomplished. This made me want to do my part, so I chose to study mechanical engineering in college. After I got my BTech degree, I joined our family business in 2002. At that time, we were making only a handful of machines, and most of the big factories liked to buy the fancier, high-tech imported machines.

At first, people just thought our machines were a cheaper choice than the ones from abroad. But I had bigger dreams. I wanted our company to be the best at making machines in India. I aimed to build machines that weren't just as good, but better and more advanced than the ones we used to import.

This ambition aligned perfectly with Prime Minister Modi's 'Make in India' initiative, which inspired me even further. I committed myself to extensive learning, taking specialized courses in machine design, hydraulics, and electrical systems. I was determined to stay abreast of the latest technologies, always thinking, researching, and striving for improvement. The journey was filled with trial and error, a series of challenges to overcome, but I stayed the course, driven by a vision of excellence and national pride.

Throughout our journey, we've not only met but also surpassed many milestones, establishing ourselves as the top footwear sole machinery manufacturer in India. We proudly offer a line of machines that represent the pinnacle of industry innovation and operational efficiency. As innovators in the Indian market, we have introduced an extensive range of machinery, including pioneering developments in single, double, and triple color sole and insole machines, along with EVA hot and cold presses—all industry firsts in India.

Our dedication to quality and innovation has garnered us a strong client base of over 600 satisfied customers, and we have sold more than 1420 machines to date. A remarkable indicator of our success is that some of our clients have up to 80 stations of our machinery running in a single factory. This level of client commitment highlights the trust in our brand and the proven performance of our products in high-demand production settings.

Why I Wrote This Book?

As a business owner, I am incredibly grateful for the love and support that my customers have shown me throughout my journey. Their loyalty and trust have been instrumental in the growth and success of my business. As a result, I feel a strong sense of responsibility to give back to them in any way that I can.

One of the ways through which I aspire to fulfil this responsibility is by educating my customers about my products, services, and the industry at large. Over the years, I have gained a wealth of knowledge and experience in the field of sole moulding, and I believe that this knowledge can prove invaluable to my clients. By sharing my expertise and insights, I hope to help my customers achieve greater profitability and success within their own businesses.

At the heart of my approach lies a commitment to building strong and lasting relationships with my clients. I believe that trust and transparency are essential to any successful partnership, and I am always striving to deepen the bond between myself and my customers. By consistently providing exceptional value and surpassing their expectations at every turn, I aspire to foster an enduring sense of loyalty and trust that will withstand the test of time.

Of course, this is not an easy task. It requires a deep understanding of my clients' needs, as well as a willingness to go above and beyond to fulfil those needs. However, after two decades of experience in the industry, I have learned that this is the only way to truly succeed in this industry. By putting my customers first and making their success my top priority, I am confident in my ability to make a positive impact in their lives and help them achieve their goals. And that, to me, is the ultimate reward.

Why you should read this book?

Maximising profits from an injection moulding machine requires:

- Optimizing production processes for efficiency and cost-effectiveness.

- Utilizing the machine to its full capacity and minimizing idle time.

- Continuously monitoring and reducing production costs.

- Maintaining high-quality standards to reduce waste and rework.

- Pursuing excellence in all aspects of production.

I hope that by reading this book, you'll gain invaluable insights into the sole moulding process and equip yourself with practical and effective methods to take your business to new heights. Transform your approach and elevate your success with this informative and impactful guide.

Who Should Read This Book?

Audience

- **Sole Manufacturers:**

  This book is a valuable resource for manufacturers specifically involved in the production of soles. Whether you operate on a small-scale or large-scale, the insights and knowledge shared in this book will empower you to make informed decisions when selecting sole moulding machines. It provides guidance on optimising operations, improving efficiency, and maximizing profits within the realm of sole manufacturing. Whether you are new to the industry or looking to enhance your existing processes, this book will offer practical strategies and tips to help you succeed.

- **Production Engineers and Technicians:**

  Production engineers and technicians responsible for operating and maintaining sole moulding machines will benefit from the technical insights provided in this book. It covers topics such as machine selection, setup and maintenance, ensuring smooth operations and minimising downtime in the sole manufacturing process.

- **Entrepreneurs and Startups:**

  If you are an entrepreneur or planning to start a sole manufacturing business, this book is a comprehensive guide that will be of immense value to you. It offers valuable advice on setting up a factory, choosing the right equipment, and effectively addressing the unique challenges associated with the sole moulding. Gain a solid foundation in the industry and avoid common pitfalls.

Brief about the Indian Footwear market and its Growth Potential

The Indian footwear market is witnessing rapid growth and intense competition, fueled by a substantial and growing population, increasing disposable incomes, and changing fashion trends. The market is highly fragmented, with both organised and unorganised players operating in the space. Within the organised segment, a handful of major players such as Bata, Adidas, Nike, Puma, and Reebok dominate the market, while the unorganised segment is dominated by small and medium-sized players that cater to the lower end of the market.

The Indian footwear market offers a wide range of products, including formal shoes, casual shoes, sports shoes, sandals, and slippers. With Indian consumers being highly price-sensitive, the market is fiercely competitive, with players offering products at different price points. Recognizing the industry's significance, the Indian government has been supportive of the footwear industry, providing incentives and subsidies to promote growth and exports. Moreover, the government has implemented policies to encourage the adoption of eco-friendly and sustainable materials within the footwear industry.

A lot of leather footwear is exported from India because the country is one of the largest producers of leather and leather products in the world. With a rich heritage of leather craftsmanship, the industry boasts a strong presence in the country. Additionally, the availability of skilled labour and raw materials such as leather, rubber, and other components used in shoe production makes India an attractive destination for leather footwear manufacturing.

India exports leather footwear to a wide range of countries, including the United States, the United Kingdom, Germany, France, Italy, and Japan, among others. The demand for Indian leather footwear is driven by changing fashion trends, increasing disposable incomes, and a growing preference for high-quality and eco-friendly products.

Overall, India's leather footwear exports are an important contributor to the country's economy, generating employment and foreign exchange earnings. As a growing economy, India is poised to experience tremendous growth and offer abundant opportunities for everyone in the next decade.

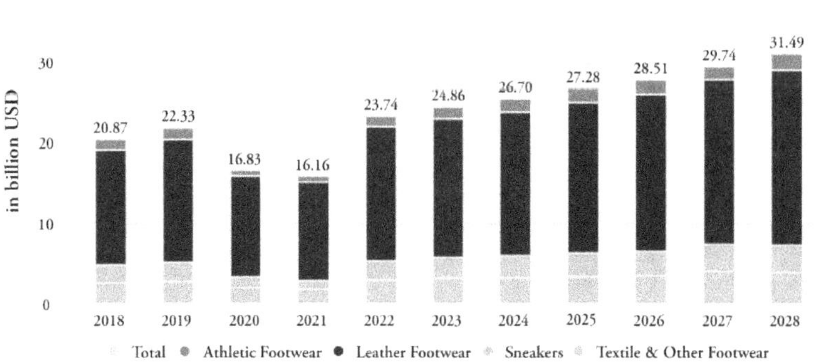

It is forecasted that the Indian footwear industry will grow at a compound annual growth rate (CAGR) of at least 12.34% over the next ten years, with an expected value of 31.49 billion US dollars.

Several factors have contributed to India's position as a leading manufacturer of shoes in the world. These factors include skilled labour, low labour costs, availability of raw materials, government support, a growing domestic market, and the adoption of advanced technology. Indian manufacturers have made investments in advanced technology and machinery to improve production efficiency and the quality of shoes, enabling them to effectively compete with other major footwear manufacturing countries in the world.

Introduction To Footwear Making

The two most prominent techniques for making footwear are adhesion moulding and direct injection. While there are various methods and materials used in shoe production, these two techniques have gained significant popularity. By exploring these methods, we can gain a basic understanding of the manufacturing processes behind footwear.

1. **Direct Injection Process (DIP)**

   The direct injection process involves fixing the shoe upper in a mould and injecting molten material to create the final shoes.

   The direct injection process offers advantages such as strong bond between the upper and sole, as well as increased production efficiency due to reduced labour involvement.

2. **Adhesion moulding (Hand Pasting)**

   The process of cementing or adhesive bonding involves attaching the sole to the upper of a shoe using specialised adhesives.

While direct injection moulding has its advantages, such as seamless bonding and intricate design, shoes with separate soles offer distinct benefits in terms of repairability, material selection, customization, and comfort-enhancing features. These factors make them a preferred choice in certain shoe categories and for consumers with specific needs.

Additionally, in direct injection moulding, designing the sole to have a bulky and elevated appearance can lead to a significant increase in weight. This is due to the limitations imposed by the moulding process, which restricts the extent of design possibilities for the sole. On the other hand, when using separate soles, it is possible to create a visually heavy and elevated appearance while keeping the weight of the sole relatively low. This enables greater flexibility in achieving the desired aesthetic without compromising the overall weight of the shoe.

Introduction to Sole Moulding

Sole moulding refers to the process of manufacturing the soles of shoes or footwear. The sole, which is the bottom part of a shoe, is responsible for providing support and protection to the foot. It is typically made from durable materials such as rubber, leather, or synthetic compounds.

Various methods are employed in sole moulding, depending on the type of shoe and the materials used. Here are a few commonly used sole moulding techniques:

Compression Moulding

In this process, a pre-measured amount of uncured rubber or other materials is placed into a mould. The mould is then subjected to heat, and pressure, causing it to compress and take on the desired shape. Through the curing process, the material solidifies, resulting in a durable sole.

Injection Moulding

Injection moulding is a widely used manufacturing process for plastic products, including footwear soles. In this method, raw material pellets are melted and injected into a precision-machined mould cavity under high pressure. As the material cools and solidifies within the mould, intricate sole shapes are achieved. Injection moulding offers notable advantages in terms of precision, complexity, speed, and efficiency, facilitating the production of intricate shapes and high volumes with minimal waste.

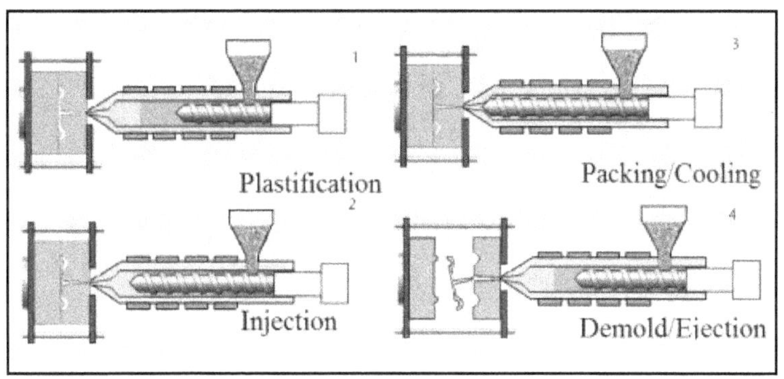

https://tscplasma.com/laser-direct-structure

Extrusion Moulding

Extrusion moulding is a widely used process in the footwear industry for creating midsoles, outsoles, and other components. It involves melting raw material pellets (like TPR, TPU, or PVC) and extruding them through a die to form the desired shape.

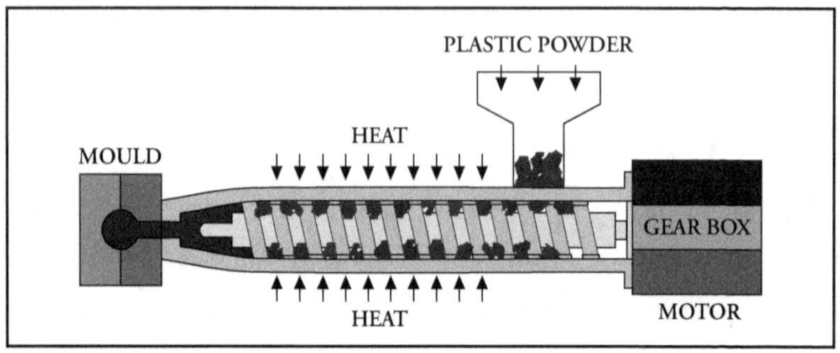

PLASTIC POWDER
HEAT
MOULD
GEAR BOX
MOTOR
HEAT

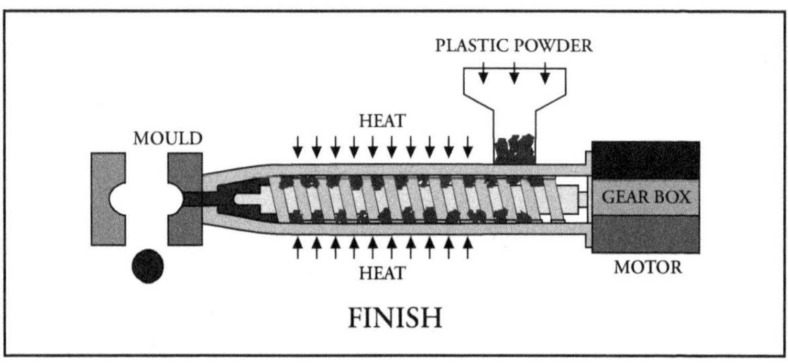

PLASTIC POWDER
HEAT
MOULD
GEAR BOX
MOTOR
HEAT
FINISH

From Research To Purchase

A 10-Step Plan to buy the Perfect Sole Machine

Last week, a client from Narela visited my factory with the intention of purchasing a machine. During our conversation, he shared his unfortunate experience of falling victim to a scam, resulting in a significant loss of two years. He was tricked by a man promising to make a cheaper alternative machine. Sadly, the client believed him and ended up losing money, wasting time, missing out on opportunities, and enduring considerable stress. Reflecting upon his situation, he expressed regret and wished he had chosen to purchase my machine earlier, avoiding the unfortunate scam altogether.

Over the past 21 years in business, I have observed numerous instances where people have been misled and ultimately deceived when buying machines. They often make mistakes because they focus too much on the price differences rather than conducting thorough background checks before making their decisions.

Let's break the process in 10 simple steps

Step 1: Identifying Your Specific Requirements

Before embarking on your search, it is crucial to have a clear understanding of your specific requirements. What type of soles are you looking to produce? How many units do you plan to manufacture daily or weekly? These specifications will serve as a guiding framework in your pursuit of the suitable machine. They will form a blueprint for the machinery characteristics you need, such as production capacity, operational efficiency, and raw material compatibility.

Step 2: Start Your Search

Once you've outlined your needs, the next stage involves conducting a thorough online search to identify potential machinery suppliers. Utilize platforms like Google, Indiamart, and Justdial, as they serve as excellent starting points. Additionally, draw upon your past experiences from industry exhibitions, conversations with fellow manufacturers, and any references provided by raw material suppliers. The objective at this stage is to compile a comprehensive list of potential suppliers.

Step 3: Connecting With Potential Suppliers and Asking the Right Questions

After compiling your list, the next logical step is to initiate contact with these suppliers. Inquire about the specific details of their machines. Ask questions that align with your requirements outlined in step 1. Whenever feasible, request demonstration videos to gain a better understanding of the machines in action. Questions should revolve around production capacity, electricity load, space requirements, operator requirements, cost of production, machine features, as well as the types of products and raw materials compatible with the machine.

Step 4: Scheduling Visits and Machine Demonstrations

Now, it's time to visit these suppliers in person. This stage is crucial in assessing their capabilities and the functionality of their machines. Insist on a live demonstration, and don't forget to ask for a list of their past clients. During the demonstration, actively engage with the machine operators and ask direct questions about machine performance, ease of operation, service support, and any potential issues that may arise. Before leaving, ensure that you request a formal quotation from the supplier.

Step 5: Conducting a Background Check on the Suppliers

Once you have narrowed down your choices, carry out a thorough background check on your potential suppliers. Reach out to their past customers to gather genuine reviews and feedback. Additionally, visit their websites and search for testimonials To gather further insights. Remember, information is power. The more you know about a supplier's reputation and track record, the more informed your final decision will be.

Step 6: Evaluating the Return on Investment (ROI)

This step involves focusing on the numbers. It is crucial to ensure that your investment is financially viable. To assess this, forecast the potential profits that the machine could generate and calculate the return on investment. If your calculations indicate that the machine could pay for itself in less than two years, it's generally considered a good investment.

Step 7: Final Decision - Selecting the Supplier

Having completed the due diligence, it's now time to make a decision. Choose a supplier based on the factors that matter the most: machine efficiency, supplier expertise, supplier reputation, after-sales service, and supplier experience. Don't forget, the price should be the last factor considered, not the initial one.

Step 8: Negotiating the Price

With your supplier chosen, it's time to discuss the price. Be tactful and fair in your negotiation. While it is important to seek a favorable deal, pushing too hard might result in a compromise on machine quality.

Step 9: Documentation - Agreement and Terms

When you've agreed on a price, make sure to document all the specifications and terms of the purchase. This documentation should include details such as the delivery date, loading charges, freight insurance, and any other relevant terms. It is advisable to keep a copy of this agreement for future reference and clarification.

Step 10: Regular Communication Until Delivery

From the agreement stage until the delivery, maintain regular communication with the supplier. Regular follow-ups help ensure a smoother delivery process and keep you in the loop about any updates or changes.

In conclusion, choosing the appropriate sole moulding machine isn't just about making a purchase but a strategic investment that directly impacts the success of your production line. By identifying your requirements, conducting thorough research, calculating the return on investment (ROI), and maintaining open communication with your chosen supplier, you are positioning your business for long-term success. The dedication and diligence invested in this process are sure to yield benefits far beyond the mere acquisition of a machine.

After finalising the machine, the next step is to select the right ancillary equipment that is compatible with the machine.

Selecting The Right
Ancillary Equipment

To produce high-quality TPR soles using a moulding machine, the selection of suitable ancillary equipment is crucial. Ancillary equipment, such as material preheaters, mixers, and conveyors, plays a vital role in ensuring the consistent quality of the TPR material before it is moulded. This is essential because consistent quality is directly related to customer satisfaction and can help establish a reputation for producing reliable and durable products. By investing in the right ancillary equipment, manufacturers can ensure that their TPR soles are consistently of high quality, which can help attract and retain customers in a highly competitive market.

Waste Cutter Selection Guide...

Selecting the appropriate waste cutter or grinder is essential for optimal performance and efficiency. These are available in various sizes and configurations, with the two primary types being straight blade grinders and staggered blade grinders.

Traditional straight blade grinders employ a single elongated blade, typically made from Old Kamani, within a cast body. This conventional design has been widely used in many industries for its simplicity.

Staggered blade grinders, on the other hand, represent a more contemporary approach to grinding. They are fitted with angular blades, made from Die steel D3, housed in a mild steel machined body. This innovative design rotates in a circular pattern, delivering efficient grinding at a faster rate compared to straight blade counterparts. Furthermore, this setup helps in reducing the electric motor kW requirement, making it a highly energy-efficient solution.

When considering factors like noise level, power usage, and grinding efficiency, staggered blade grinders excel. They offer versatility by being suitable for both continuous and batch grinding. Unique features, such as an easy blade-changing mechanism and adjustable blades, enable quick replacements and facilitate cutting of diverse materials, respectively. This adaptability reduces downtime, decreases replacement costs, and enhances productivity, making staggered blade grinders an excellent choice for various grinding needs.

SELECTING THE HYDRAULIC OIL FOR THE MACHINE

Seven years ago, a customer located in Narela purchased a new machine from us. After the installation was completed, the customer reached out to me and reported that the machine was producing unusual sounds. I was surprised to hear this and, therefore, dispatched an engineer to the customer's factory to identify the issue. The engineer discovered that the customer had procured substandard oil that was too viscous, causing excessive load on the machine's pump. We advised the customer to replace the oil, and subsequently, the machine operated smoothly. It is not uncommon for customers to make mistakes in selecting the appropriate hydraulic oil for their machine. Often, they purchase from local vendors who mix oils, or buy cheap imported oils that are unsuitable for operating machinery.

Hydraulic oil plays a vital role in injection moulding machines as it transfers energy and applies force to hydraulic components. It lubricates parts, prevents wear, and ensures smooth operation. Low-quality oil can lead to decreased efficiency, increased wear and tear, contamination, poor machine performance, and reduced machine life. Therefore, high-quality oil suited for specific machine needs is crucial.

When selecting hydraulic oil for injection moulding machines, consider the following technical specifications:

- Viscosity: Ensure that the oil's viscosity suits the machine's operating conditions.

- Viscosity Index (VI): A higher VI ensures consistent performance by maintaining viscosity across temperatures.

- Anti-wear Properties: Look for oil with anti-wear additives to protect hydraulic components.

- Compatibility: Ensure that the oil is compatible with machine materials, including seals and gaskets.

- Rust and Corrosion Protection: Choose oil with rust and corrosion inhibitors for hydraulic system protection.

Conclusion

Therefore, it is essential to choose a hydraulic oil with a good TOST life, rust test, and viscosity index, as these factors can impact the performance and durability of your hydraulic equipment. Additionally, consider the manufacturer's recommendations and consult with an expert to ensure that you are selecting the appropriate hydraulic oil for your machine.

The L.E.A.P. Framework

Acquiring a machine and putting it to use are two distinct steps. In today's competitive business world, it is crucial to be efficient and attentive. Otherwise, your business may struggle to generate sufficient revenue or fail to achieve anticipated growth. Running a business can be demanding, as various challenges often create disorder and uncertainty.

Life as a business owner can be challenging. You might face many problems that cause a lot of confusion. Through my interactions with various business owners, I realized that most of the problems in businesses are common and happen over and over again. I thought that I could do something to help them.

After years of dedicated hard work and leveraging the knowledge acquired from 21 years of experience, I discovered a set of solutions That could assist business professionals in reducing their stress and increasing their profits. I named this framework the LEAP framework.

Now, let's discuss what the LEAP framework is. We will break it down and explain each part, enabling you to understand how it can benefit both you and your business. With the right information and a bit of hard work, you can utilize the LEAP framework to improve your business.

L. Lower down time

Have you ever experienced a situation where, just as you receive some orders, the machine operator informs you of a sudden breakdown caused by an unexpected fault? With an urgent order on your hands, the fear and tension of how to explain the situation to your client and the possibility of failing to meet your commitment can be very stressful.

We will learn how to avoid such situations by considering the example of a car, which is also a machine and is even more complex than a sole moulding machine.

Many of us use or drive a car, and breakdowns are rare. This is because we regularly maintain and service our cars. At fixed intervals, we take our cars to a service station where a service advisor goes through a checklist, ensuring that all points are covered. We need to adopt this same method and apply it to our machines.

Ask your machinery supplier to provide you with a maintenance manual or checklist that is needed for preventive maintenance.

Typical preventive maintenance checks required in a TPR sole machine:

Maintenance Task	Frequency
Oiling and greasing of tie rods and Bush blocks	Every 14 days
Cleaning of oil cooler pipes	Every 90-120 days, Depending upon water type
Cleaning the cooling plates where the mould is fitted	Every 60 days
Checking hydraulic oil and gear oil levels	Every 30 days
Filtration of hydraulic oil	Every year
Replacement of hydraulic oil	Every 2-3 years of operation
Cleaning of hydraulic oil filter	Every 1 month
Replacing Gear Oil	Every 250 hours of operation

Please contact the machine manufacturer for the full detailed checklist of the preventive maintenance checks required.

Preventive maintenance for moulding machines involves regular activities to prevent equipment failure. This proactive approach includes routine checks, cleaning, lubrication, and replacing worn parts to avoid downtime and keep the machine working well. Regular cleaning and lubrication are also crucial. Regular preventive maintenance can help avoid unexpected failures, loss of production time, poor product quality, and high repair costs. Additionally, it helps extend the machine's life, ensuring it runs efficiently for a longer time.

Since a factory may have various machines and models, keeping track of maintenance checklists and their implementation on the factory floor can be challenging. To simplify this, we've introduced an automated WhatsApp messaging system that sends reminders about upcoming maintenance checks.

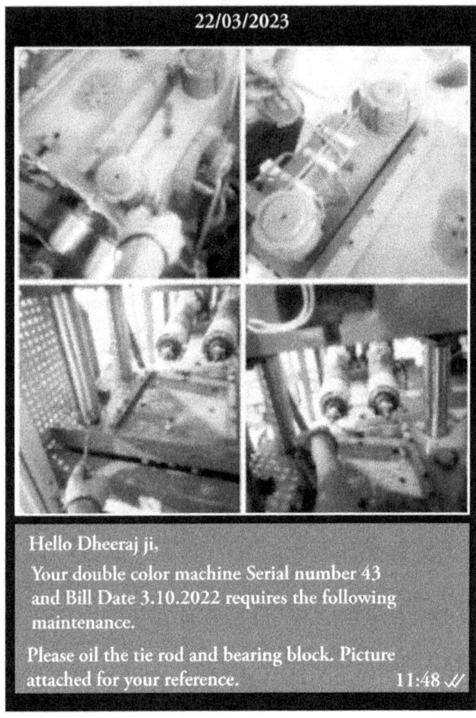

A sample message sent automatically to our client for periodic maintenance.

In conclusion, preventive maintenance is an essential aspect of TPR moulding machine maintenance that helps to ensure smooth and efficient operation, preventing unexpected downtime, reducing repair costs, and extending the lifespan of the equipment.

E. Energy Efficiency

In today's world, energy efficiency has become a critical factor in the selection of machinery. Energy-efficient machines are designed to consume less energy while maintaining their functionality, making them a beneficial choice for both the environment and your finances. Moreover, it's not only new machines that can achieve energy efficiency. Even older machines can be retrofitted to achieve improved efficiency through targeted enhancements, such as the integration of Variable Frequency Drives (VFDs) and energy-efficient heaters. These upgrades can significantly reduce the energy consumption of existing machinery, resulting in substantial energy cost savings over time. Therefore, whether you are purchasing new equipment or optimizing existing ones, the focus should always be on prioritizing energy efficiency.

VFD (Variable Frequency Drives)

One of the primary features that defines an energy-efficient machine is its ability to adapt its energy consumption according to the task at hand. This is where the variable frequency drives (VFD) come into the picture. VFDs are devices that can control the speed of an electric motor, which is the primary energy-consuming component in most machines. By varying the speed of the motor, VFDs can ensure that only the required energy is consumed, thereby reducing energy waste and associated costs.

Energy Saving Ceramic Heaters

Another critical factor to consider when selecting an energy-efficient machine is the heating system it employs. Efficient heating systems are designed to convert the maximum amount of input energy into heat output. This is typically achieved through advanced heaters such as energy-saving ceramic types instead of conventional mica types. It has been observed that these heaters can save up to 20-40% in electricity consumption. By choosing a machine with an efficient heating system, you can save on energy costs and reduce the environmental impact associated with energy consumption.

In conclusion, the adoption of energy-efficient technologies, such as Variable Frequency Drives (VFDs) and energy-saving heaters, can lead to substantial reductions in the energy consumption of existing machinery. By retrofitting older equipment with these advanced features, we can optimize their performance and significantly reduce electricity usage. VFDs provide precise control over motor speed and torque, thereby enhancing machine efficiency, while energy-efficient heaters contribute to overall power savings. This transformative approach offers a practical and cost-effective solution that promotes sustainability and helps achieve cost reductions. As we conclude this chapter on energy-saving, it is evident that implementing strategic updates to our machinery represents a significant step toward our energy conservation goals.

A. Advance Training

One day, a client called me requesting assistance in finding a new operator for our sole moulding machine. When I inquired about the reason for needing a new operator, he explained that the previous operator's negligence had resulted in the rejection of an entire lot of soles intended for a shoe exporter.

When it comes to operator experience, running a TPR sole moulding machine can present several challenges.. One of the primary concerns is a lack of training or experience, which can lead to errors in machine operation, resulting in subpar product quality or even damage to the machine. Inexperienced operators may also face difficulties in adjusting machine settings, such as temperature and pressure, in order to achieve optimal performance. Additionally, operators may not be familiar with the proper maintenance procedures, leading to neglected maintenance that can cause machine breakdowns and downtime.

To address these issues, it is important to provide adequate training and support to operators, ensuring they possess the necessary skills and knowledge to operate and maintain the machine effectively. This can be accomplished by putting up a Training system in the organisation.

This can be achieved by implementing a four-step training system for operators running a TPR sole moulding machine:

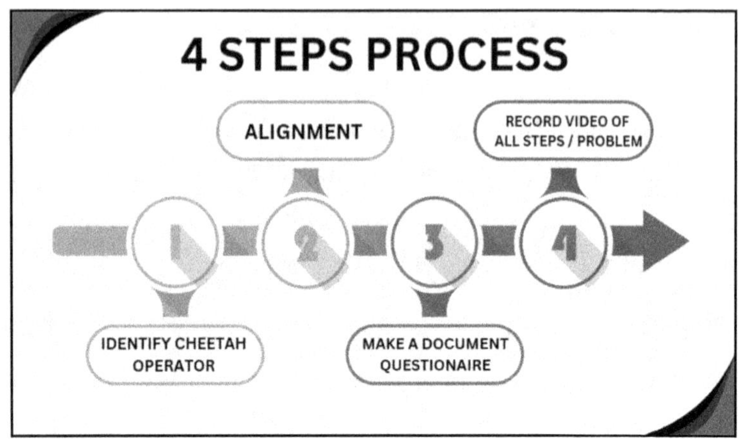

Step 1: Identify cheetah operator

Identify the best operator in the company who possesses in-depth knowledge and skills necessary for operating the machine effectively. These skills may include machine setup, material preparation, machine operation, quality control, and maintenance.

Step 2: Alignment

You should sit down with him and align your thoughts, as he may be hesitant to share all his expertise required for the training program. Often, they might fear that the owner could let them go once the training system is established. This concern can result in them providing unclear or incomplete responses during the creation of the training system. It's crucial to convince him of the benefits he will gain from the training process. Assure him that he will be featured in all the training videos and will become a prominent figure in the company, garnering respect from everyone.

Step 3: Make a detailed questionnaire

Next, create a questionnaire that includes all questions relevant to the training you're conducting. The more questions you have, the more thorough your results will be. You could ask things like: How do you start the machine? How do you change the mould? What are the required heating temperatures for the machine? What should you do if the sole has burn marks or if there's a shortage of filled soles? In essence, your questionnaire should be detailed and all-encompassing, covering even the smallest aspects.

Step 4: Creating Videos

Next, take each point from the questionnaire and start creating videos to cover them all. These videos should be in a simple, local language that the machine operator can easily understand. You can then merge these videos to create longer ones for different sections and upload them to a private YouTube channel, keeping them unlisted.

Now, since problems and solutions are ever-evolving, it is important to keep updating the questionnaire and videos as new issues arise and new solutions are discovered.

Encourage ongoing learning and development by providing opportunities for operators to continue to building their skills and knowledge over time. This can be achieved through refresher training sessions, workshops, and other professional development opportunities.

By following these steps, you can develop a comprehensive training system that helps operators effectively operate a TPR sole moulding machine, leading to improved product quality and reduced downtime.

P. Performance Upgradation

Often, we receive requests for TPU soles or Expanded TPR soles. However, we generally can't meet these demands because there's a common belief that we need screw piston machines to process these polymers. As a result, we decline these profitable projects. But with specific modifications to the machine, we can process these polymers. Let's delve into the process of TPU.

To process TPU, it is necessary to preheat the granules to approximately 90 degrees Celsius, and it should be processed at a temperature of 170 degrees for the best outcome. If we introduce the material at 170 degrees into the hooper, the motor struggles to extrude TPU into the mould due to the machine being overloaded. This problem occurs because we are using a screw that is designed for processing TPR, not TPU.

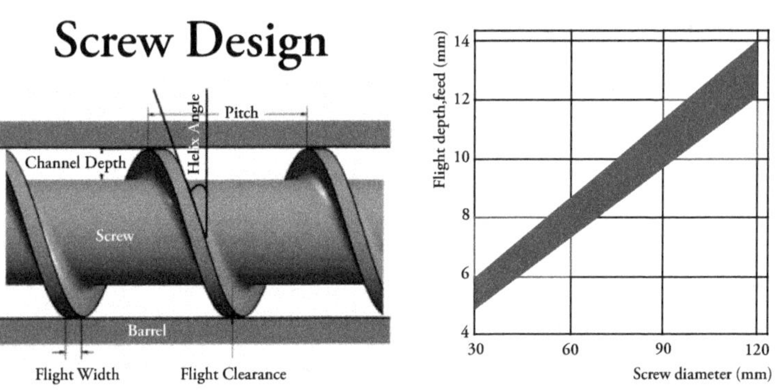

Relationship between screw diameter and flight depth at feed

The graph indicates that the depth of a 66 mm screw near the feeding zone should be about 8.5 mm. However, for typical TPR screws, depth is around 12-13 mm. So, if we adjust the screw depth from 12-13 mm to align with the compression ratio specified by the material supplier, we can efficiently process TPU with our machines. Additionally,, we need to decrease the revolutions per minute (rpm) of the screw, which can be achieved with a Variable Frequency Drive (VFD).

When it comes to processing Expanded Thermoplastic Rubber (TPR), a different approach is required. Expanded TPR needs to be injected into the mould at a high rotational speed, ensuring that the necessary expansion happens right inside the mould itself. To make this possible, we need to significantly increase the rotations per minute (rpm) of the screw. Specifically, we must raise the screw rpm to somewhere around 280-300 rpm.

The reason for this high speed is to make sure that the TPR material is able to expand appropriately while inside the mould. By increasing the rpm, the screw moves faster and more forcefully, effectively pushing the material into the mould with the necessary force to initiate the expansion process. As a result, Expanded TPR soles with the desired texture and features are created.

So, with the right adjustments to the machine parameters, we can also successfully process Expanded TPR, extending the range of products we can offer to our clients.

Conclusion

In the book "The Sole of Success", we've taken an exciting and enlightening journey into the world of sole manufacturing factories. Starting with a brief about the promising Indian Footwear market, we've delved into the intricacies of footwear making and the specifics of sole moulding.

The chapters have been structured to guide you right from research to the final purchase of your ideal sole machine, presenting you with a practical and effective 10-step plan. We also addressed the crucial task of selecting the right ancillary equipment, including the selection guide for a waste cutter and choosing the appropriate hydraulic oil for your machine.

A standout feature of this book is the L.E.A.P. framework, which serves as a guiding light for achieving success in this industry. This innovative concept aids you in lowering downtime, improving energy efficiency, providing advance training for your team, and facilitating equipment performance upgrades.

The strategies and techniques outlined in this book are not mere theoretical concepts; they are the result of extensive experience and practical wisdom. These insights have the power to revolutionize your business operations, ultimately resulting in improved efficiency, cost reduction, and increased profitability.

Whether you're a seasoned professional in this industry or someone planning to venture into it, this book offers you a treasure trove of invaluable insights and practical guidance. By embracing the knowledge presented in "The Sole of Success", you are indeed setting yourself on the path to achieving significant growth and profitability in the sole manufacturing business. Thank you for joining me on this enlightening journey. Always remember, success is within your reach - it all starts with a single step, or in our case, a sole.

The Author Closing Remark

Dear Reader,

Thank you for embarking on this journey with me and investing your time in reading my book. I hope it has provided you with valuable insights and knowledge to enhance your manufacturing endeavours.

Although I have made an effort to cover various aspects of sole manufacturing in this book, I understand that every business faces unique challenges and encounters specific issues that may not be addressed comprehensively within these pages. Therefore, I extend an invitation to connect with me personally so that we can delve deeper into your individual problems and find tailored solutions together.

Feel free to reach out to me via WhatsApp at my number, +91 9911504010. Simply provide a brief overview of the challenges you are currently facing, and we can schedule a discussion to analyse your specific problems, audit your existing machinery and operations, and develop effective solutions.

As a gesture of appreciation, please consider filling out the form below to receive automated reminders for preventive maintenance messages on WhatsApp for one year. These reminders can help ensure that your equipment remains in good working condition, reducing the risk of breakdowns and improving the quality of your product. Thank you for your interest and commitment to maintaining your equipment.

Additionally, I invite you to connect with me on LinkedIn, where I regularly share valuable insights, industry updates, and strategies to fuel business growth. By connecting on LinkedIn, you will have the opportunity to join a dynamic community of like-minded professionals who share similar interests and stay updated with the latest advancements in the footwear industry.

Thank you once again for being a part of this journey. I look forward to connecting with you and working together to overcome your manufacturing obstacles.

Best regards,

Shagun Banga

   📞 +91 9911504010

   ✉ md@technocratmachines.com

    www.linkedin.com/in/shagunbanga/

Or scan the code below to add my profile:

For free 1-year preventive maintenance reminders on WhatsApp, scan or click the link below.

NOTES:

NOTES:

* 9 7 8 9 3 5 5 5 4 5 7 1 8 *